DANCING

Written by
Lynn Trepicchio

Illustrated by
Stéphan Daigle

HARCOURT BRACE & COMPANY

Orlando Atlanta Austin Boston San Francisco Chicago Dallas New York
Toronto London

Dancing is tapping with your toes.

Dancing is leaping through the air.

Dancing is moving your legs and arms.

Dancing is acting on a stage.